IT'S TIME TO EAT APPLE PIE

It's Time to Eat
APPLE PIE

Walter the Educator

Silent King Books
A WhichHead Entertainment Imprint

Copyright © 2024 by Walter the Educator

All rights reserved. No part of this book may be reproduced in any manner whatsoever without written per- mission except in the case of brief quotations embodied in critical articles and reviews.

First Printing, 2024

Disclaimer

This book is a literary work; the story is not about specific persons, locations, situations, and/or circumstances unless mentioned in a historical context. Any resemblance to real persons, locations, situations, and/or circumstances is coincidental. This book is for entertainment and informational purposes only. The author and publisher offer this information without warranties expressed or implied. No matter the grounds, neither the author nor the publisher will be accountable for any losses, injuries, or other damages caused by the reader's use of this book. The use of this book acknowledges an understanding and acceptance of this disclaimer.

It's Time to Eat APPLE PIE is a collectible early learning book by Walter the Educator suitable for all ages belonging to Walter the Educator's Time to Eat Book Series. Collect more books at WaltertheEducator.com

USE THE EXTRA SPACE TO TAKE NOTES AND DOCUMENT YOUR MEMORIES

APPLE PIE

Apple pie, apple pie, golden and round,

It's Time to Eat
Apple Pie

A warm little treasure that I just found.

Crust so flaky, apples so sweet,

A yummy treat that's hard to beat.

With a slice on my plate, warm and nice,

I grab my fork and don't think twice.

The apples inside are soft and gooey,

With cinnamon spice, warm and chewy.

Take a sniff, oh, what a smell!

Like cozy fall days, I know so well.

It's time to taste, just one small bite,

Apple pie feels just right!

Some like it with a scoop of cream,

Or with ice cream that makes it gleam.

But even plain, it's such a treat,

Apple pie is fun to eat!

It's Time to Eat
Apple Pie

Baked in the oven, golden and warm,

Each slice of pie is a tasty charm.

With apples inside, tart and sweet,

It's a comfort food we love to eat.

Crunchy, chewy, soft, and smooth,

Apple pie puts us in a good mood.

For breakfast or dessert at night,

Apple pie is always right!

From the orchard, apples we pick,

Red and green, juicy and thick.

Baked with love, with care and cheer,

Apple pie time is finally here!

It's time to share a slice or two,

With friends and family, just for you.

A pie for all, a pie to share,

It's Time to Eat
Apple Pie

Apple pie shows how much we care.

The crust on top, so warm and brown,

The best little treat in all the town.

Take a big bite, give it a try,

Nothing's better than apple pie!

So gather around, and take a seat,

Apple pie is ready to eat.

Each bite is joy, each taste is fun,

It's Time to Eat
Apple Pie

Apple pie for everyone!

ABOUT THE CREATOR

Walter the Educator is one of the pseudonyms for Walter Anderson. Formally educated in Chemistry, Business, and Education, he is an educator, an author, a diverse entrepreneur, and he is the son of a disabled war veteran. "Walter the Educator" shares his time between educating and creating. He holds interests and owns several creative projects that entertain, enlighten, enhance, and educate, hoping to inspire and motivate you. Follow, find new works, and stay up to date with Walter the Educator™

at WaltertheEducator.com

Milton Keynes UK
Ingram Content Group UK Ltd.
UKHW022115251124
451529UK00012B/520